Name of Look _____

Evening ○

Daytime ○

Face

Moisturizer

Concealer

Foundation

Highlight/Blush

Eyes

Brows

Eyelid

Liner

Crease

Mascara

Lips

Liner

Lip Color

Gloss

Notes

Name of Look _____

Evening ◯

Daytime ◯

Face

Moisturizer

Concealer

Foundation

Highlight/Blush

Eyes

Brows

Eyelid

Liner

Crease

Mascara

Lips

Liner

Lip Color

Gloss

Notes

Name of Look _____

Evening ◯

Daytime ◯

Face

Moisturizer

Concealer

Foundation

Highlight/Blush

Eyes

Brows

Eyelid

Liner

Crease

Mascara

Lips

Liner

Lip Color

Gloss

Notes

Name of Look _____

Evening ○

Daytime ○

Face

Moisturizer

Concealer

Foundation

Highlight/Blush

Eyes

Brows

Eyelid

Liner

Crease

Mascara

Lips

Liner

Lip Color

Gloss

Notes

Name of Look _____

Evening ○

Daytime ○

Face

Moisturizer

Concealer

Foundation

Highlight/Blush

Eyes

Brows

Eyelid

Liner

Crease

Mascara

Lips

Liner

Lip Color

Gloss

Notes

Name of Look _____

Evening ○

Daytime ○

Face

Moisturizer
_____

Concealer
_____

Foundation
_____

Highlight/Blush
_____

Eyes

Brows
_____

Eyelid
_____

Liner
_____

Crease
_____

Mascara
_____

Lips

Liner
_____

Lip Color
_____

Gloss
_____

Notes

Name of Look _____

Evening ○

Daytime ○

Face

Moisturizer

Concealer

Foundation

Highlight/Blush

Eyes

Brows

Eyelid

Liner

Crease

Mascara

Lips

Liner

Lip Color

Gloss

Notes

Name of Look _____

Evening ○

Daytime ○

Face

Moisturizer

Concealer

Foundation

Highlight/Blush

Eyes

Brows

Eyelid

Liner

Crease

Mascara

Lips

Liner

Lip Color

Gloss

Notes

Name of Look _____

Evening ○

Daytime ○

Face

Moisturizer

Concealer

Foundation

Highlight/Blush

Eyes

Brows

Eyelid

Liner

Crease

Mascara

Lips

Liner

Lip Color

Gloss

Notes

Name of Look _____

Evening ○

Daytime ○

Face

Moisturizer

_____

Concealer

_____

Foundation

_____

Highlight/Blush

_____

Eyes

Brows

_____

Eyelid

_____

Liner

_____

Crease

_____

Mascara

Lips

Liner

_____

Lip Color

_____

Gloss

Notes

Name of Look _____

Evening ◯

Daytime ◯

Face

Moisturizer
_____

Concealer
_____

Foundation
_____

Highlight/Blush
_____

Eyes

Brows
_____

Eyelid
_____

Liner
_____

Crease
_____

Mascara
_____

Lips

Liner
_____

Lip Color
_____

Gloss
_____

Notes

Name of Look _____

Evening ○

Daytime ○

Face

Moisturizer

_____

Concealer

_____

Foundation

_____

Highlight/Blush

_____

Eyes

Brows

_____

Eyelid

_____

Liner

_____

Crease

_____

Mascara

_____

Lips

Liner

_____

Lip Color

_____

Gloss

_____

Notes

Name of Look _____

Evening ○

Daytime ○

Face

Moisturizer

Concealer

Foundation

Highlight/Blush

Eyes

Brows

Eyelid

Liner

Crease

Mascara

Lips

Liner

Lip Color

Gloss

Notes

Name of Look _____

Evening ○

Daytime ○

Face

Moisturizer
_____

Concealer
_____

Foundation
_____

Highlight/Blush
_____

Eyes

Brows
_____

Eyelid
_____

Liner
_____

Crease
_____

Mascara
_____

Lips

Liner
_____

Lip Color
_____

Gloss
_____

Notes

Name of Look _____

Evening ○

Daytime ○

Face

Moisturizer

Concealer

Foundation

Highlight/Blush

Eyes

Brows

Eyelid

Liner

Crease

Mascara

Lips

Liner

Lip Color

Gloss

Notes

Name of Look _____

Evening ○

Daytime ○

Face

Moisturizer

_____

Concealer

_____

Foundation

_____

Highlight/Blush

_____

Eyes

Brows

_____

Eyelid

_____

Liner

_____

Crease

_____

Mascara

_____

Lips

Liner

_____

Lip Color

_____

Gloss

_____

Notes

Name of Look _____

Evening ◯

Daytime ◯

Face

Moisturizer

Concealer

Foundation

Highlight/Blush

Eyes

Brows

Eyelid

Liner

Crease

Mascara

Lips

Liner

Lip Color

Gloss

Notes

Name of Look _____

Evening ○

Daytime ○

Face

Moisturizer

_____

Concealer

_____

Foundation

_____

Highlight/Blush

_____

Eyes

Brows

_____

Eyelid

_____

Liner

_____

Crease

_____

Mascara

Lips

Liner

_____

Lip Color

_____

Gloss

_____

Notes

Name of Look _____

Evening ○

Daytime ○

Face

Moisturizer

Concealer

Foundation

Highlight/Blush

Eyes

Brows

Eyelid

Liner

Crease

Mascara

Lips

Liner

Lip Color

Gloss

Notes

Name of Look _____

Evening ○

Daytime ○

Face

Moisturizer

_____

Concealer

_____

Foundation

_____

Highlight/Blush

_____

Eyes

Brows

_____

Eyelid

_____

Liner

_____

Crease

_____

Mascara

Lips

Liner

_____

Lip Color

_____

Gloss

Notes

Name of Look _____

Evening ○

Daytime ○

Face

Moisturizer

Concealer

Foundation

Highlight/Blush

Eyes

Brows

Eyelid

Liner

Crease

Mascara

Lips

Liner

Lip Color

Gloss

Notes

Name of Look _____

Evening ○

Daytime ○

Face

Moisturizer
_____

Concealer
_____

Foundation
_____

Highlight/Blush
_____

Eyes

Brows
_____

Eyelid
_____

Liner
_____

Crease
_____

Mascara
_____

Lips

Liner
_____

Lip Color
_____

Gloss
_____

Notes

Name of Look _____

Evening ○

Daytime ○

Face

Moisturizer

Concealer

Foundation

Highlight/Blush

Eyes

Brows

Eyelid

Liner

Crease

Mascara

Lips

Liner

Lip Color

Gloss

Notes

Name of Look _____

Evening ○

Daytime ○

Face

Moisturizer
_____

Concealer
_____

Foundation
_____

Highlight/Blush
_____

Eyes

Brows
_____

Eyelid
_____

Liner
_____

Crease
_____

Mascara
_____

Lips

Liner
_____

Lip Color
_____

Gloss
_____

Notes

Name of Look _____

Evening ○

Daytime ○

Face

Moisturizer

Concealer

Foundation

Highlight/Blush

Eyes

Brows

Eyelid

Liner

Crease

Mascara

Lips

Liner

Lip Color

Gloss

Notes

Name of Look _____

Evening ○

Daytime ○

Face

Moisturizer

Concealer

Foundation

Highlight/Blush

Eyes

Brows

Eyelid

Liner

Crease

Mascara

Lips

Liner

Lip Color

Gloss

Notes

Name of Look _____

Evening ○

Daytime ○

Face

Moisturizer

Concealer

Foundation

Highlight/Blush

Eyes

Brows

Eyelid

Liner

Crease

Mascara

Lips

Liner

Lip Color

Gloss

Notes

Name of Look _____

Evening ○

Daytime ○

Face

Moisturizer

Concealer

Foundation

Highlight/Blush

Eyes

Brows

Eyelid

Liner

Crease

Mascara

Lips

Liner

Lip Color

Gloss

Notes

Name of Look _____

Evening ○

Daytime ○

Face

Moisturizer

Concealer

Foundation

Highlight/Blush

Eyes

Brows

Eyelid

Liner

Crease

Mascara

Lips

Liner

Lip Color

Gloss

Notes

Name of Look _____

Evening ○

Daytime ○

Face

Moisturizer
_____

Concealer
_____

Foundation
_____

Highlight/Blush
_____

Eyes

Brows
_____

Eyelid
_____

Liner
_____

Crease
_____

Mascara
_____

Lips

Liner
_____

Lip Color
_____

Gloss
_____

Notes

Name of Look _____

Evening ○

Daytime ○

Face

Moisturizer

Concealer

Foundation

Highlight/Blush

Eyes

Brows

Eyelid

Liner

Crease

Mascara

Lips

Liner

Lip Color

Gloss

Notes

Name of Look _____

Evening ○

Daytime ○

Face

Moisturizer

Concealer

Foundation

Highlight/Blush

Eyes

Brows

Eyelid

Liner

Crease

Mascara

Lips

Liner

Lip Color

Gloss

Notes

Name of Look _____

Evening ○

Daytime ○

Face

Moisturizer

Concealer

Foundation

Highlight/Blush

Eyes

Brows

Eyelid

Liner

Crease

Mascara

Lips

Liner

Lip Color

Gloss

Notes

Name of Look _____

Evening ○

Daytime ○

Face

Moisturizer
_____

Concealer
_____

Foundation
_____

Highlight/Blush
_____

Eyes

Brows
_____

Eyelid
_____

Liner
_____

Crease
_____

Mascara

Lips

Liner
_____

Lip Color
_____

Gloss
_____

Notes

Name of Look _____

Evening ○

Daytime ○

Face

Moisturizer

Concealer

Foundation

Highlight/Blush

Eyes

Brows

Eyelid

Liner

Crease

Mascara

Lips

Liner

Lip Color

Gloss

Notes

Name of Look _____

Evening ○

Daytime ○

Face

Moisturizer

Concealer

Foundation

Highlight/Blush

Eyes

Brows

Eyelid

Liner

Crease

Mascara

Lips

Liner

Lip Color

Gloss

Notes

Name of Look _____

Evening ○

Daytime ○

Face

Moisturizer

Concealer

Foundation

Highlight/Blush

Eyes

Brows

Eyelid

Liner

Crease

Mascara

Lips

Liner

Lip Color

Gloss

Notes

Name of Look _____

Evening ○

Daytime ○

Face

Moisturizer
_____

Concealer
_____

Foundation
_____

Highlight/Blush
_____

Eyes

Brows
_____

Eyelid
_____

Liner
_____

Crease
_____

Mascara
_____

Lips

Liner
_____

Lip Color
_____

Gloss
_____

Notes

Name of Look _____

Evening ○

Daytime ○

Face

Moisturizer

Concealer

Foundation

Highlight/Blush

Eyes

Brows

Eyelid

Liner

Crease

Mascara

Lips

Liner

Lip Color

Gloss

Notes

Name of Look _____

Evening ○

Daytime ○

Face

Moisturizer

Concealer

Foundation

Highlight/Blush

Eyes

Brows

Eyelid

Liner

Crease

Mascara

Lips

Liner

Lip Color

Gloss

Notes

Name of Look _____

Evening ○

Daytime ○

Face

Moisturizer

Concealer

Foundation

Highlight/Blush

Eyes

Brows

Eyelid

Liner

Crease

Mascara

Lips

Liner

Lip Color

Gloss

Notes

Name of Look _____

Evening ○

Daytime ○

Face

Moisturizer
_____

Concealer
_____

Foundation
_____

Highlight/Blush
_____

Eyes

Brows
_____

Eyelid
_____

Liner
_____

Crease
_____

Mascara
_____

Lips

Liner
_____

Lip Color
_____

Gloss
_____

Notes

Name of Look _____

Evening ○

Daytime ○

Face

Moisturizer

Concealer

Foundation

Highlight/Blush

Eyes

Brows

Eyelid

Liner

Crease

Mascara

Lips

Liner

Lip Color

Gloss

Notes

Name of Look _____

Evening ○

Daytime ○

Face

Moisturizer

Concealer

Foundation

Highlight/Blush

Eyes

Brows

Eyelid

Liner

Crease

Mascara

Lips

Liner

Lip Color

Gloss

Notes

Name of Look _____

Evening ○

Daytime ○

Face

Moisturizer

Concealer

Foundation

Highlight/Blush

Eyes

Brows

Eyelid

Liner

Crease

Mascara

Lips

Liner

Lip Color

Gloss

Notes

Name of Look _____

Evening ○

Daytime ○

Face

Moisturizer

Concealer

Foundation

Highlight/Blush

Eyes

Brows

Eyelid

Liner

Crease

Mascara

Lips

Liner

Lip Color

Gloss

Notes

Name of Look _____

Evening ○
Daytime ○

Face

Moisturizer

Concealer

Foundation

Highlight/Blush

Eyes

Brows

Eyelid

Liner

Crease

Mascara

Lips

Liner

Lip Color

Gloss

Notes

Name of Look _____

Evening ○

Daytime ○

Face

Moisturizer

_____

Concealer

_____

Foundation

_____

Highlight/Blush

_____

Eyes

Brows

_____

Eyelid

_____

Liner

_____

Crease

_____

Mascara

_____

Lips

Liner

_____

Lip Color

_____

Gloss

_____

Notes

Name of Look _____

Evening ○

Daytime ○

Face

Moisturizer

Concealer

Foundation

Highlight/Blush

Eyes

Brows

Eyelid

Liner

Crease

Mascara

Lips

Liner

Lip Color

Gloss

Notes

Name of Look _____

Evening ○

Daytime ○

Face

Moisturizer

___

Concealer

___

Foundation

___

Highlight/Blush

___

Eyes

Brows

___

Eyelid

___

Liner

___

Crease

___

Mascara

Lips

Liner

___

Lip Color

___

Gloss

Notes

Name of Look _____

Evening ○

Daytime ○

Face

Moisturizer

Concealer

Foundation

Highlight/Blush

Eyes

Brows

Eyelid

Liner

Crease

Mascara

Lips

Liner

Lip Color

Gloss

Notes

Name of Look _____

Evening ○

Daytime ○

Face

Moisturizer
_____

Concealer
_____

Foundation
_____

Highlight/Blush
_____

Eyes

Brows
_____

Eyelid
_____

Liner
_____

Crease
_____

Mascara

Lips

Liner
_____

Lip Color
_____

Gloss
_____

Notes

Name of Look _____

Evening ○
Daytime ○

Face

Moisturizer

Concealer

Foundation

Highlight/Blush

Eyes

Brows

Eyelid

Liner

Crease

Mascara

Lips

Liner

Lip Color

Gloss

Notes

Name of Look _____

Evening ○

Daytime ○

Face

Moisturizer
_____

Concealer
_____

Foundation
_____

Highlight/Blush
_____

Eyes

Brows
_____

Eyelid
_____

Liner
_____

Crease
_____

Mascara
_____

Lips

Liner
_____

Lip Color
_____

Gloss
_____

Notes

Name of Look _____

Evening ○

Daytime ○

Face

Moisturizer

Concealer

Foundation

Highlight/Blush

Eyes

Brows

Eyelid

Liner

Crease

Mascara

Lips

Liner

Lip Color

Gloss

Notes

Name of Look _____

Evening ○

Daytime ○

Face

Moisturizer

___

Concealer

___

Foundation

___

Highlight/Blush

___

Eyes

Brows

___

Eyelid

___

Liner

___

Crease

___

Mascara

___

Lips

Liner

___

Lip Color

___

Gloss

Notes

Name of Look _____

Evening ○

Daytime ○

Face

Moisturizer

Concealer

Foundation

Highlight/Blush

Eyes

Brows

Eyelid

Liner

Crease

Mascara

Lips

Liner

Lip Color

Gloss

Notes

Name of Look _____

Evening ○

Daytime ○

Face

Moisturizer
_____

Concealer
_____

Foundation
_____

Highlight/Blush
_____

Eyes

Brows
_____

Eyelid
_____

Liner
_____

Crease
_____

Mascara
_____

Lips

Liner
_____

Lip Color
_____

Gloss
_____

Notes

Name of Look _____

Evening ○

Daytime ○

Face

Moisturizer

Concealer

Foundation

Highlight/Blush

Eyes

Brows

Eyelid

Liner

Crease

Mascara

Lips

Liner

Lip Color

Gloss

Notes

Name of Look _____

Evening ○

Daytime ○

Face

Moisturizer
_____

Concealer
_____

Foundation
_____

Highlight/Blush
_____

Eyes

Brows
_____

Eyelid
_____

Liner
_____

Crease
_____

Mascara

Lips

Liner
_____

Lip Color
_____

Gloss
_____

Notes

Name of Look _____

Evening ○

Daytime ○

Face

Moisturizer

Concealer

Foundation

Highlight/Blush

Eyes

Brows

Eyelid

Liner

Crease

Mascara

Lips

Liner

Lip Color

Gloss

Notes

Name of Look _____

Evening ○

Daytime ○

Face

Moisturizer

Concealer

Foundation

Highlight/Blush

Eyes

Brows

Eyelid

Liner

Crease

Mascara

Lips

Liner

Lip Color

Gloss

Notes

Name of Look _____

Evening ○

Daytime ○

Face

Moisturizer

Concealer

Foundation

Highlight/Blush

Eyes

Brows

Eyelid

Liner

Crease

Mascara

Lips

Liner

Lip Color

Gloss

Notes

Name of Look _____

Evening ○

Daytime ○

Face

Moisturizer

Concealer

Foundation

Highlight/Blush

Eyes

Brows

Eyelid

Liner

Crease

Mascara

Lips

Liner

Lip Color

Gloss

Notes

Name of Look _____

Evening ○

Daytime ○

Face

Moisturizer

Concealer

Foundation

Highlight/Blush

Eyes

Brows

Eyelid

Liner

Crease

Mascara

Lips

Liner

Lip Color

Gloss

Notes

Name of Look _____

Evening ○

Daytime ○

Face

Moisturizer

Concealer

Foundation

Highlight/Blush

Eyes

Brows

Eyelid

Liner

Crease

Mascara

Lips

Liner

Lip Color

Gloss

Notes

Name of Look _____

Evening ○

Daytime ○

Face

Moisturizer

Concealer

Foundation

Highlight/Blush

Eyes

Brows

Eyelid

Liner

Crease

Mascara

Lips

Liner

Lip Color

Gloss

Notes

Name of Look _____

Evening ○

Daytime ○

Face

Moisturizer

Concealer

Foundation

Highlight/Blush

Eyes

Brows

Eyelid

Liner

Crease

Mascara

Lips

Liner

Lip Color

Gloss

Notes

Name of Look _____

Evening ○

Daytime ○

Face

Moisturizer

Concealer

Foundation

Highlight/Blush

Eyes

Brows

Eyelid

Liner

Crease

Mascara

Lips

Liner

Lip Color

Gloss

Notes

Name of Look _____

Evening ○

Daytime ○

Face

Moisturizer

_____

Concealer

_____

Foundation

_____

Highlight/Blush

_____

Eyes

Brows

_____

Eyelid

_____

Liner

_____

Crease

_____

Mascara

_____

Lips

Liner

_____

Lip Color

_____

Gloss

_____

Notes

Name of Look _____

Evening ○

Daytime ○

Face

Moisturizer

Concealer

Foundation

Highlight/Blush

Eyes

Brows

Eyelid

Liner

Crease

Mascara

Lips

Liner

Lip Color

Gloss

Notes

Name of Look _____

Evening ○

Daytime ○

Face

Moisturizer
_____

Concealer
_____

Foundation
_____

Highlight/Blush
_____

Eyes

Brows
_____

Eyelid
_____

Liner
_____

Crease
_____

Mascara
_____

Lips

Liner
_____

Lip Color
_____

Gloss
_____

Notes

Name of Look _____

Evening ◯

Daytime ◯

Face

Moisturizer

Concealer

Foundation

Highlight/Blush

Eyes

Brows

Eyelid

Liner

Crease

Mascara

Lips

Liner

Lip Color

Gloss

Notes

Name of Look _____

Evening ○

Daytime ○

Face

Moisturizer

Concealer

Foundation

Highlight/Blush

Eyes

Brows

Eyelid

Liner

Crease

Mascara

Lips

Liner

Lip Color

Gloss

Notes

Name of Look _____

Evening ○

Daytime ○

Face

Moisturizer

Concealer

Foundation

Highlight/Blush

Eyes

Brows

Eyelid

Liner

Crease

Mascara

Lips

Liner

Lip Color

Gloss

Notes

Name of Look _____

Evening ○

Daytime ○

Face

Moisturizer

Concealer

Foundation

Highlight/Blush

Eyes

Brows

Eyelid

Liner

Crease

Mascara

Lips

Liner

Lip Color

Gloss

Notes

Name of Look _____

Evening ○

Daytime ○

Face

Moisturizer

Concealer

Foundation

Highlight/Blush

Eyes

Brows

Eyelid

Liner

Crease

Mascara

Lips

Liner

Lip Color

Gloss

Notes

Name of Look _____

Evening ○

Daytime ○

Face

Moisturizer
_____

Concealer
_____

Foundation
_____

Highlight/Blush
_____

Eyes

Brows
_____

Eyelid
_____

Liner
_____

Crease
_____

Mascara
_____

Lips

Liner
_____

Lip Color
_____

Gloss
_____

Notes

Name of Look _____

Evening ○

Daytime ○

Face

Moisturizer

Concealer

Foundation

Highlight/Blush

Eyes

Brows

Eyelid

Liner

Crease

Mascara

Lips

Liner

Lip Color

Gloss

Notes

Name of Look _____

Evening ○

Daytime ○

Face

Moisturizer
_____

Concealer
_____

Foundation
_____

Highlight/Blush
_____

Eyes

Brows
_____

Eyelid
_____

Liner
_____

Crease
_____

Mascara

Lips

Liner
_____

Lip Color
_____

Gloss
_____

Notes

Name of Look _____

Evening ○

Daytime ○

Face

Moisturizer

Concealer

Foundation

Highlight/Blush

Eyes

Brows

Eyelid

Liner

Crease

Mascara

Lips

Liner

Lip Color

Gloss

Notes

Name of Look _____

Evening ○

Daytime ○

Face

Moisturizer
_____

Concealer
_____

Foundation
_____

Highlight/Blush
_____

Eyes

Brows
_____

Eyelid
_____

Liner
_____

Crease
_____

Mascara

Lips

Liner
_____

Lip Color
_____

Gloss
_____

Notes

Name of Look _____

Evening ○

Daytime ○

Face

Moisturizer

Concealer

Foundation

Highlight/Blush

Eyes

Brows

Eyelid

Liner

Crease

Mascara

Lips

Liner

Lip Color

Gloss

Notes

Name of Look _____

Evening ○

Daytime ○

Face

Moisturizer

Concealer

Foundation

Highlight/Blush

Eyes

Brows

Eyelid

Liner

Crease

Mascara

Lips

Liner

Lip Color

Gloss

Notes

Name of Look _____

Evening ○

Daytime ○

Face

Moisturizer

Concealer

Foundation

Highlight/Blush

Eyes

Brows

Eyelid

Liner

Crease

Mascara

Lips

Liner

Lip Color

Gloss

Notes

Name of Look _____

Evening ○

Daytime ○

Face

Moisturizer
_____

Concealer
_____

Foundation
_____

Highlight/Blush
_____

Eyes

Brows
_____

Eyelid
_____

Liner
_____

Crease
_____

Mascara
_____

Lips

Liner
_____

Lip Color
_____

Gloss
_____

Notes

Name of Look _____

Evening ○

Daytime ○

Face

Moisturizer

Concealer

Foundation

Highlight/Blush

Eyes

Brows

Eyelid

Liner

Crease

Mascara

Lips

Liner

Lip Color

Gloss

Notes

Name of Look _____

Evening ○

Daytime ○

Face

Moisturizer

Concealer

Foundation

Highlight/Blush

Eyes

Brows

Eyelid

Liner

Crease

Mascara

Lips

Liner

Lip Color

Gloss

Notes

Name of Look _____

Evening ○

Daytime ○

Face

Moisturizer

Concealer

Foundation

Highlight/Blush

Eyes

Brows

Eyelid

Liner

Crease

Mascara

Lips

Liner

Lip Color

Gloss

Notes

Name of Look _____

Evening ○

Daytime ○

Face

Moisturizer

Concealer

Foundation

Highlight/Blush

Eyes

Brows

Eyelid

Liner

Crease

Mascara

Lips

Liner

Lip Color

Gloss

Notes

Name of Look _____

Evening ○

Daytime ○

Face

Moisturizer

Concealer

Foundation

Highlight/Blush

Eyes

Brows

Eyelid

Liner

Crease

Mascara

Lips

Liner

Lip Color

Gloss

Notes

Name of Look _____

Evening ○

Daytime ○

Face

Moisturizer

Concealer

Foundation

Highlight/Blush

Eyes

Brows

Eyelid

Liner

Crease

Mascara

Lips

Liner

Lip Color

Gloss

Notes

Name of Look _____

Evening ○

Daytime ○

Face

Moisturizer

Concealer

Foundation

Highlight/Blush

Eyes

Brows

Eyelid

Liner

Crease

Mascara

Lips

Liner

Lip Color

Gloss

Notes

Name of Look _____

Evening ○

Daytime ○

Face

Moisturizer

Concealer

Foundation

Highlight/Blush

Eyes

Brows

Eyelid

Liner

Crease

Mascara

Lips

Liner

Lip Color

Gloss

Notes

Name of Look _____

Evening ○

Daytime ○

Face

Moisturizer

Concealer

Foundation

Highlight/Blush

Eyes

Brows

Eyelid

Liner

Crease

Mascara

Lips

Liner

Lip Color

Gloss

Notes

Name of Look _____

Evening ○

Daytime ○

Face

Moisturizer

Concealer

Foundation

Highlight/Blush

Eyes

Brows

Eyelid

Liner

Crease

Mascara

Lips

Liner

Lip Color

Gloss

Notes

Name of Look _____

Evening ○

Daytime ○

Face

Moisturizer

Concealer

Foundation

Highlight/Blush

Eyes

Brows

Eyelid

Liner

Crease

Mascara

Lips

Liner

Lip Color

Gloss

Notes

Name of Look _____

Evening ○

Daytime ○

Face

Moisturizer

Concealer

Foundation

Highlight/Blush

Eyes

Brows

Eyelid

Liner

Crease

Mascara

Lips

Liner

Lip Color

Gloss

Notes

Name of Look _____

Evening ○

Daytime ○

Face

Moisturizer

Concealer

Foundation

Highlight/Blush

Eyes

Brows

Eyelid

Liner

Crease

Mascara

Lips

Liner

Lip Color

Gloss

Notes

Name of Look _____

Evening ◯

Daytime ◯

Face

Moisturizer

Concealer

Foundation

Highlight/Blush

Eyes

Brows

Eyelid

Liner

Crease

Mascara

Lips

Liner

Lip Color

Gloss

Notes

Name of Look _____

Evening ○

Daytime ○

Face

Moisturizer

Concealer

Foundation

Highlight/Blush

Eyes

Brows

Eyelid

Liner

Crease

Mascara

Lips

Liner

Lip Color

Gloss

Notes

Name of Look _____

Evening ○

Daytime ○

Face

Moisturizer

Concealer

Foundation

Highlight/Blush

Eyes

Brows

Eyelid

Liner

Crease

Mascara

Lips

Liner

Lip Color

Gloss

Notes

Name of Look _____

Evening ○

Daytime ○

Face

Moisturizer

Concealer

Foundation

Highlight/Blush

Eyes

Brows

Eyelid

Liner

Crease

Mascara

Lips

Liner

Lip Color

Gloss

Notes

Name of Look _____

Evening ○

Daytime ○

Face

Moisturizer

Concealer

Foundation

Highlight/Blush

Eyes

Brows

Eyelid

Liner

Crease

Mascara

Lips

Liner

Lip Color

Gloss

Notes

Name of Look _____

Evening ○

Daytime ○

Face

Moisturizer

Concealer

Foundation

Highlight/Blush

Eyes

Brows

Eyelid

Liner

Crease

Mascara

Lips

Liner

Lip Color

Gloss

Notes

Name of Look _____

Evening ○

Daytime ○

Face

Moisturizer
_____

Concealer
_____

Foundation
_____

Highlight/Blush
_____

Eyes

Brows
_____

Eyelid
_____

Liner
_____

Crease
_____

Mascara
_____

Lips

Liner
_____

Lip Color
_____

Gloss
_____

Notes

Name of Look _____

Evening ○

Daytime ○

Face

Moisturizer

Concealer

Foundation

Highlight/Blush

Eyes

Brows

Eyelid

Liner

Crease

Mascara

Lips

Liner

Lip Color

Gloss

Notes

Name of Look _____

Evening ○

Daytime ○

Face

Moisturizer

Concealer

Foundation

Highlight/Blush

Eyes

Brows

Eyelid

Liner

Crease

Mascara

Lips

Liner

Lip Color

Gloss

Notes

Name of Look _____

Evening ◯

Daytime ◯

Face

Moisturizer

Concealer

Foundation

Highlight/Blush

Eyes

Brows

Eyelid

Liner

Crease

Mascara

Lips

Liner

Lip Color

Gloss

Notes

Name of Look _____

Evening ○

Daytime ○

Face

Moisturizer

Concealer

Foundation

Highlight/Blush

Eyes

Brows

Eyelid

Liner

Crease

Mascara

Lips

Liner

Lip Color

Gloss

Notes

Name of Look _____

Evening ○

Daytime ○

Face

Moisturizer

Concealer

Foundation

Highlight/Blush

Eyes

Brows

Eyelid

Liner

Crease

Mascara

Lips

Liner

Lip Color

Gloss

Notes

Name of Look _____

Evening ○

Daytime ○

Face

Moisturizer

Concealer

Foundation

Highlight/Blush

Eyes

Brows

Eyelid

Liner

Crease

Mascara

Lips

Liner

Lip Color

Gloss

Notes

Name of Look _____

Evening ○

Daytime ○

Face

Moisturizer

Concealer

Foundation

Highlight/Blush

Eyes

Brows

Eyelid

Liner

Crease

Mascara

Lips

Liner

Lip Color

Gloss

Notes

Name of Look _____

Evening ○

Daytime ○

Face

Moisturizer

_____

Concealer

_____

Foundation

_____

Highlight/Blush

_____

Eyes

Brows

_____

Eyelid

_____

Liner

_____

Crease

_____

Mascara

_____

Lips

Liner

_____

Lip Color

_____

Gloss

_____

Notes

Name of Look _____

Evening ○

Daytime ○

Face

Moisturizer
_____

Concealer
_____

Foundation
_____

Highlight/Blush
_____

Eyes

Brows
_____

Eyelid
_____

Liner
_____

Crease
_____

Mascara
_____

Lips

Liner
_____

Lip Color
_____

Gloss
_____

Notes

Name of Look _____

Evening ○

Daytime ○

Face

Moisturizer
_____

Concealer
_____

Foundation
_____

Highlight/Blush
_____

Eyes

Brows
_____

Eyelid
_____

Liner
_____

Crease
_____

Mascara

Lips

Liner
_____

Lip Color
_____

Gloss
_____

Notes

Name of Look _____

Evening ○

Daytime ○

Face

Moisturizer

Concealer

Foundation

Highlight/Blush

Eyes

Brows

Eyelid

Liner

Crease

Mascara

Lips

Liner

Lip Color

Gloss

Notes

Name of Look _____

Evening ○

Daytime ○

Face

Moisturizer
_____

Concealer
_____

Foundation
_____

Highlight/Blush
_____

Eyes

Brows
_____

Eyelid
_____

Liner
_____

Crease
_____

Mascara
_____

Lips

Liner
_____

Lip Color
_____

Gloss
_____

Notes

Name of Look _____

Evening ○

Daytime ○

Face

Moisturizer

Concealer

Foundation

Highlight/Blush

Eyes

Brows

Eyelid

Liner

Crease

Mascara

Lips

Liner

Lip Color

Gloss

Notes

Name of Look _____

Evening ○

Daytime ○

Face

Moisturizer

Concealer

Foundation

Highlight/Blush

Eyes

Brows

Eyelid

Liner

Crease

Mascara

Lips

Liner

Lip Color

Gloss

Notes

Name of Look _____

Evening ◯

Daytime ◯

Face

Moisturizer
_____

Concealer
_____

Foundation
_____

Highlight/Blush
_____

Eyes

Brows
_____

Eyelid
_____

Liner
_____

Crease
_____

Mascara

Lips

Liner
_____

Lip Color
_____

Gloss
_____

Notes

Name of Look _____

Evening ○

Daytime ○

Face

Moisturizer
_____

Concealer
_____

Foundation
_____

Highlight/Blush
_____

Eyes

Brows
_____

Eyelid
_____

Liner
_____

Crease
_____

Mascara
_____

Lips

Liner
_____

Lip Color
_____

Gloss
_____

Notes

Name of Look _____

Evening ○

Daytime ○

Face

Moisturizer

Concealer

Foundation

Highlight/Blush

Eyes

Brows

Eyelid

Liner

Crease

Mascara

Lips

Liner

Lip Color

Gloss

Notes

Name of Look _____

Evening ○

Daytime ○

Face

Moisturizer

Concealer

Foundation

Highlight/Blush

Eyes

Brows

Eyelid

Liner

Crease

Mascara

Lips

Liner

Lip Color

Gloss

Notes

Name of Look _____

Evening ○

Daytime ○

Face

Moisturizer

Concealer

Foundation

Highlight/Blush

Eyes

Brows

Eyelid

Liner

Crease

Mascara

Lips

Liner

Lip Color

Gloss

Notes

Name of Look _____

Evening ○

Daytime ○

Face

Moisturizer
_____

Concealer
_____

Foundation
_____

Highlight/Blush
_____

Eyes

Brows
_____

Eyelid
_____

Liner
_____

Crease
_____

Mascara
_____

Lips

Liner
_____

Lip Color
_____

Gloss
_____

Notes

Name of Look _____

Evening ○

Daytime ○

Face

Moisturizer

Concealer

Foundation

Highlight/Blush

Eyes

Brows

Eyelid

Liner

Crease

Mascara

Lips

Liner

Lip Color

Gloss

Notes

Name of Look _____

Evening ○

Daytime ○

Face

Moisturizer

Concealer

Foundation

Highlight/Blush

Eyes

Brows

Eyelid

Liner

Crease

Mascara

Lips

Liner

Lip Color

Gloss

Notes

Name of Look _____

Evening ○

Daytime ○

Face

Moisturizer

Concealer

Foundation

Highlight/Blush

Eyes

Brows

Eyelid

Liner

Crease

Mascara

Lips

Liner

Lip Color

Gloss

Notes

Name of Look _____

Evening ○

Daytime ○

Face

Moisturizer

Concealer

Foundation

Highlight/Blush

Eyes

Brows

Eyelid

Liner

Crease

Mascara

Lips

Liner

Lip Color

Gloss

Notes

Name of Look _____

Evening ○

Daytime ○

Face

Moisturizer

Concealer

Foundation

Highlight/Blush

Eyes

Brows

Eyelid

Liner

Crease

Mascara

Lips

Liner

Lip Color

Gloss

Notes

Name of Look _____

Evening ○

Daytime ○

Face

Moisturizer

Concealer

Foundation

Highlight/Blush

Eyes

Brows

Eyelid

Liner

Crease

Mascara

Lips

Liner

Lip Color

Gloss

Notes

Name of Look _____

Evening ○

Daytime ○

Face

Moisturizer

Concealer

Foundation

Highlight/Blush

Eyes

Brows

Eyelid

Liner

Crease

Mascara

Lips

Liner

Lip Color

Gloss

Notes

Name of Look _____

Evening ○

Daytime ○

Face

Moisturizer

Concealer

Foundation

Highlight/Blush

Eyes

Brows

Eyelid

Liner

Crease

Mascara

Lips

Liner

Lip Color

Gloss

Notes

Name of Look _____

Evening ◯

Daytime ◯

Face

Moisturizer

Concealer

Foundation

Highlight/Blush

Eyes

Brows

Eyelid

Liner

Crease

Mascara

Lips

Liner

Lip Color

Gloss

Notes

Name of Look _____

Evening ○

Daytime ○

Face

Moisturizer

Concealer

Foundation

Highlight/Blush

Eyes

Brows

Eyelid

Liner

Crease

Mascara

Lips

Liner

Lip Color

Gloss

Notes

Name of Look _____

Evening ○

Daytime ○

Face

Moisturizer

Concealer

Foundation

Highlight/Blush

Eyes

Brows

Eyelid

Liner

Crease

Mascara

Lips

Liner

Lip Color

Gloss

Notes

Name of Look _____

Evening ○

Daytime ○

Face

Moisturizer

Concealer

Foundation

Highlight/Blush

Eyes

Brows

Eyelid

Liner

Crease

Mascara

Lips

Liner

Lip Color

Gloss

Notes

Name of Look _____

Evening ○

Daytime ○

Face

Moisturizer

Concealer

Foundation

Highlight/Blush

Eyes

Brows

Eyelid

Liner

Crease

Mascara

Lips

Liner

Lip Color

Gloss

Notes

Name of Look _____

Evening ○

Daytime ○

Face

Moisturizer

Concealer

Foundation

Highlight/Blush

Eyes

Brows

Eyelid

Liner

Crease

Mascara

Lips

Liner

Lip Color

Gloss

Notes

Name of Look _____

Evening ○

Daytime ○

Face

Moisturizer

Concealer

Foundation

Highlight/Blush

Eyes

Brows

Eyelid

Liner

Crease

Mascara

Lips

Liner

Lip Color

Gloss

Notes

Name of Look _____

Evening ○

Daytime ○

Face

Moisturizer

Concealer

Foundation

Highlight/Blush

Eyes

Brows

Eyelid

Liner

Crease

Mascara

Lips

Liner

Lip Color

Gloss

Notes

Name of Look _____

Evening ○

Daytime ○

Face

Moisturizer

Concealer

Foundation

Highlight/Blush

Eyes

Brows

Eyelid

Liner

Crease

Mascara

Lips

Liner

Lip Color

Gloss

Notes

Name of Look _____

Evening ○

Daytime ○

Face

Moisturizer

Concealer

Foundation

Highlight/Blush

Eyes

Brows

Eyelid

Liner

Crease

Mascara

Lips

Liner

Lip Color

Gloss

Notes

Name of Look _____

Evening ○

Daytime ○

Face

Moisturizer

Concealer

Foundation

Highlight/Blush

Eyes

Brows

Eyelid

Liner

Crease

Mascara

Lips

Liner

Lip Color

Gloss

Notes

Name of Look _____

Evening ○

Daytime ○

Face

Moisturizer
_____

Concealer
_____

Foundation
_____

Highlight/Blush
_____

Eyes

Brows
_____

Eyelid
_____

Liner
_____

Crease
_____

Mascara

Lips

Liner
_____

Lip Color
_____

Gloss
_____

Notes

Name of Look _____

Evening ○

Daytime ○

Face

Moisturizer

Concealer

Foundation

Highlight/Blush

Eyes

Brows

Eyelid

Liner

Crease

Mascara

Lips

Liner

Lip Color

Gloss

Notes

Name of Look _____

Evening ○

Daytime ○

Face

Moisturizer
_____

Concealer
_____

Foundation
_____

Highlight/Blush
_____

Eyes

Brows
_____

Eyelid
_____

Liner
_____

Crease
_____

Mascara
_____

Lips

Liner
_____

Lip Color
_____

Gloss
_____

Notes

Name of Look _____

Evening ○
Daytime ○

Face

Moisturizer

Concealer

Foundation

Highlight/Blush

Eyes

Brows

Eyelid

Liner

Crease

Mascara

Lips

Liner

Lip Color

Gloss

Notes

Name of Look _____

Evening ○

Daytime ○

Face

Moisturizer
_____

Concealer
_____

Foundation
_____

Highlight/Blush
_____

Eyes

Brows
_____

Eyelid
_____

Liner
_____

Crease
_____

Mascara

Lips

Liner
_____

Lip Color
_____

Gloss
_____

Notes

Name of Look _____

Evening ○

Daytime ○

Face

Moisturizer

Concealer

Foundation

Highlight/Blush

Eyes

Brows

Eyelid

Liner

Crease

Mascara

Lips

Liner

Lip Color

Gloss

Notes

Name of Look _____

Evening ◯

Daytime ◯

Face

Moisturizer
_____

Concealer
_____

Foundation
_____

Highlight/Blush
_____

Eyes

Brows
_____

Eyelid
_____

Liner
_____

Crease
_____

Mascara

Lips

Liner
_____

Lip Color
_____

Gloss
_____

Notes

Name of Look _____

Evening ○

Daytime ○

Face

Moisturizer

Concealer

Foundation

Highlight/Blush

Eyes

Brows

Eyelid

Liner

Crease

Mascara

Lips

Liner

Lip Color

Gloss

Notes

Name of Look _____

Evening ○

Daytime ○

Face

Moisturizer

_____

Concealer

_____

Foundation

_____

Highlight/Blush

_____

Eyes

Brows

_____

Eyelid

_____

Liner

_____

Crease

_____

Mascara

Lips

Liner

_____

Lip Color

_____

Gloss

_____

Notes

Name of Look _____

Evening ○

Daytime ○

Face

Moisturizer

Concealer

Foundation

Highlight/Blush

Eyes

Brows

Eyelid

Liner

Crease

Mascara

Lips

Liner

Lip Color

Gloss

Notes

Name of Look _____

Evening ○

Daytime ○

Face

Moisturizer
_____

Concealer
_____

Foundation
_____

Highlight/Blush
_____

Eyes

Brows
_____

Eyelid
_____

Liner
_____

Crease
_____

Mascara
_____

Lips

Liner
_____

Lip Color
_____

Gloss
_____

Notes

Name of Look _____

Evening ○

Daytime ○

Face

Moisturizer

Concealer

Foundation

Highlight/Blush

Eyes

Brows

Eyelid

Liner

Crease

Mascara

Lips

Liner

Lip Color

Gloss

Notes

Name of Look _____

Evening ○

Daytime ○

Face

Moisturizer

Concealer

Foundation

Highlight/Blush

Eyes

Brows

Eyelid

Liner

Crease

Mascara

Lips

Liner

Lip Color

Gloss

Notes

Name of Look _____

Evening ◯

Daytime ◯

Face

Moisturizer

Concealer

Foundation

Highlight/Blush

Eyes

Brows

Eyelid

Liner

Crease

Mascara

Lips

Liner

Lip Color

Gloss

Notes

Name of Look _____

Evening ○

Daytime ○

Face

Moisturizer

Concealer

Foundation

Highlight/Blush

Eyes

Brows

Eyelid

Liner

Crease

Mascara

Lips

Liner

Lip Color

Gloss

Notes

Name of Look _____

Evening ○

Daytime ○

Face

Moisturizer

Concealer

Foundation

Highlight/Blush

Eyes

Brows

Eyelid

Liner

Crease

Mascara

Lips

Liner

Lip Color

Gloss

Notes

Name of Look _____

Evening ○

Daytime ○

Face

Moisturizer

Concealer

Foundation

Highlight/Blush

Eyes

Brows

Eyelid

Liner

Crease

Mascara

Lips

Liner

Lip Color

Gloss

Notes

Name of Look _____

Evening ◯

Daytime ◯

Face

Moisturizer

Concealer

Foundation

Highlight/Blush

Eyes

Brows

Eyelid

Liner

Crease

Mascara

Lips

Liner

Lip Color

Gloss

Notes

Name of Look _____

Evening ○

Daytime ○

Face

Moisturizer
_____

Concealer
_____

Foundation
_____

Highlight/Blush
_____

Eyes

Brows
_____

Eyelid
_____

Liner
_____

Crease
_____

Mascara
_____

Lips

Liner
_____

Lip Color
_____

Gloss
_____

Notes

Name of Look _____

Evening ○

Daytime ○

Face

Moisturizer

Concealer

Foundation

Highlight/Blush

Eyes

Brows

Eyelid

Liner

Crease

Mascara

Lips

Liner

Lip Color

Gloss

Notes

Name of Look _____

Evening ○

Daytime ○

Face

Moisturizer
_____

Concealer
_____

Foundation
_____

Highlight/Blush
_____

Eyes

Brows
_____

Eyelid
_____

Liner
_____

Crease
_____

Mascara
_____

Lips

Liner
_____

Lip Color
_____

Gloss
_____

Notes

Name of Look _____

Evening ○

Daytime ○

Face

Moisturizer

Concealer

Foundation

Highlight/Blush

Eyes

Brows

Eyelid

Liner

Crease

Mascara

Lips

Liner

Lip Color

Gloss

Notes

Name of Look _____

Evening ○

Daytime ○

Face

Moisturizer
_____

Concealer
_____

Foundation
_____

Highlight/Blush
_____

Eyes

Brows
_____

Eyelid
_____

Liner
_____

Crease
_____

Mascara

Lips

Liner
_____

Lip Color
_____

Gloss
_____

Notes

Name of Look _____

Evening ○

Daytime ○

Face

Moisturizer

Concealer

Foundation

Highlight/Blush

Eyes

Brows

Eyelid

Liner

Crease

Mascara

Lips

Liner

Lip Color

Gloss

Notes

Name of Look _____

Evening ○

Daytime ○

Face

Moisturizer

Concealer

Foundation

Highlight/Blush

Eyes

Brows

Eyelid

Liner

Crease

Mascara

Lips

Liner

Lip Color

Gloss

Notes

Name of Look _____

Evening ◯

Daytime ◯

Face

Moisturizer

Concealer

Foundation

Highlight/Blush

Eyes

Brows

Eyelid

Liner

Crease

Mascara

Lips

Liner

Lip Color

Gloss

Notes

Name of Look _____

Evening ○

Daytime ○

Face

Moisturizer

Concealer

Foundation

Highlight/Blush

Eyes

Brows

Eyelid

Liner

Crease

Mascara

Lips

Liner

Lip Color

Gloss

Notes

Name of Look _____

Evening ○

Daytime ○

Face

Moisturizer

Concealer

Foundation

Highlight/Blush

Eyes

Brows

Eyelid

Liner

Crease

Mascara

Lips

Liner

Lip Color

Gloss

Notes

Name of Look _____

Evening ◯

Daytime ◯

Face

Moisturizer
_____

Concealer
_____

Foundation
_____

Highlight/Blush
_____

Eyes

Brows
_____

Eyelid
_____

Liner
_____

Crease
_____

Mascara
_____

Lips

Liner
_____

Lip Color
_____

Gloss
_____

Notes

Name of Look _____

Evening ○

Daytime ○

Face

Moisturizer

Concealer

Foundation

Highlight/Blush

Eyes

Brows

Eyelid

Liner

Crease

Mascara

Lips

Liner

Lip Color

Gloss

Notes

Name of Look _____

Evening ○

Daytime ○

Face

Moisturizer

Concealer

Foundation

Highlight/Blush

Eyes

Brows

Eyelid

Liner

Crease

Mascara

Lips

Liner

Lip Color

Gloss

Notes

Name of Look _____

Evening ○

Daytime ○

Face

Moisturizer

Concealer

Foundation

Highlight/Blush

Eyes

Brows

Eyelid

Liner

Crease

Mascara

Lips

Liner

Lip Color

Gloss

Notes

Name of Look _____

Evening ○

Daytime ○

Face

Moisturizer

Concealer

Foundation

Highlight/Blush

Eyes

Brows

Eyelid

Liner

Crease

Mascara

Lips

Liner

Lip Color

Gloss

Notes

Name of Look _____

Evening ○

Daytime ○

Face

Moisturizer

Concealer

Foundation

Highlight/Blush

Eyes

Brows

Eyelid

Liner

Crease

Mascara

Lips

Liner

Lip Color

Gloss

Notes

Name of Look _____

Evening ○

Daytime ○

Face

Moisturizer

Concealer

Foundation

Highlight/Blush

Eyes

Brows

Eyelid

Liner

Crease

Mascara

Lips

Liner

Lip Color

Gloss

Notes

Name of Look _____

Evening ○

Daytime ○

Face

Moisturizer

Concealer

Foundation

Highlight/Blush

Eyes

Brows

Eyelid

Liner

Crease

Mascara

Lips

Liner

Lip Color

Gloss

Notes

Name of Look _____

Evening ○

Daytime ○

Face

Moisturizer
_____

Concealer
_____

Foundation
_____

Highlight/Blush
_____

Eyes

Brows
_____

Eyelid
_____

Liner
_____

Crease
_____

Mascara
_____

Lips

Liner
_____

Lip Color
_____

Gloss
_____

Notes

Name of Look _____

Evening ○

Daytime ○

Face

Moisturizer

Concealer

Foundation

Highlight/Blush

Eyes

Brows

Eyelid

Liner

Crease

Mascara

Lips

Liner

Lip Color

Gloss

Notes

Name of Look _____

Evening ○

Daytime ○

Face

Moisturizer

Concealer

Foundation

Highlight/Blush

Eyes

Brows

Eyelid

Liner

Crease

Mascara

Lips

Liner

Lip Color

Gloss

Notes

Name of Look _____

Evening ○
Daytime ○

Face

Moisturizer

Concealer

Foundation

Highlight/Blush

Eyes

Brows

Eyelid

Liner

Crease

Mascara

Lips

Liner

Lip Color

Gloss

Notes

Name of Look _____

Evening ○

Daytime ○

Face

Moisturizer

Concealer

Foundation

Highlight/Blush

Eyes

Brows

Eyelid

Liner

Crease

Mascara

Lips

Liner

Lip Color

Gloss

Notes

Name of Look _____

Evening ○
Daytime ○

Face

Moisturizer

Concealer

Foundation

Highlight/Blush

Eyes

Brows

Eyelid

Liner

Crease

Mascara

Lips

Liner

Lip Color

Gloss

Notes

Name of Look _____

Evening ○

Daytime ○

Face

Moisturizer

Concealer

Foundation

Highlight/Blush

Eyes

Brows

Eyelid

Liner

Crease

Mascara

Lips

Liner

Lip Color

Gloss

Notes

Name of Look _____

Evening ○

Daytime ○

Face

Moisturizer

Concealer

Foundation

Highlight/Blush

Eyes

Brows

Eyelid

Liner

Crease

Mascara

Lips

Liner

Lip Color

Gloss

Notes

Name of Look _____

Evening ○

Daytime ○

Face

Moisturizer

_____

Concealer

_____

Foundation

_____

Highlight/Blush

_____

Eyes

Brows

_____

Eyelid

_____

Liner

_____

Crease

_____

Mascara

_____

Lips

Liner

_____

Lip Color

_____

Gloss

_____

Notes

Name of Look _____

Evening ○

Daytime ○

Face

Moisturizer

Concealer

Foundation

Highlight/Blush

Eyes

Brows

Eyelid

Liner

Crease

Mascara

Lips

Liner

Lip Color

Gloss

Notes

Name of Look _____

Evening ○

Daytime ○

Face

Moisturizer

Concealer

Foundation

Highlight/Blush

Eyes

Brows

Eyelid

Liner

Crease

Mascara

Lips

Liner

Lip Color

Gloss

Notes

Name of Look _____

Evening ○

Daytime ○

Face

Moisturizer

Concealer

Foundation

Highlight/Blush

Eyes

Brows

Eyelid

Liner

Crease

Mascara

Lips

Liner

Lip Color

Gloss

Notes

Name of Look _____

Evening ○

Daytime ○

Face

Moisturizer

Concealer

Foundation

Highlight/Blush

Eyes

Brows

Eyelid

Liner

Crease

Mascara

Lips

Liner

Lip Color

Gloss

Notes

Name of Look _____

Evening ○

Daytime ○

Face

Moisturizer

Concealer

Foundation

Highlight/Blush

Eyes

Brows

Eyelid

Liner

Crease

Mascara

Lips

Liner

Lip Color

Gloss

Notes

Name of Look _____

Evening ○

Daytime ○

Face

Moisturizer

Concealer

Foundation

Highlight/Blush

Eyes

Brows

Eyelid

Liner

Crease

Mascara

Lips

Liner

Lip Color

Gloss

Notes

Name of Look _____

Evening ○

Daytime ○

Face

Moisturizer

Concealer

Foundation

Highlight/Blush

Eyes

Brows

Eyelid

Liner

Crease

Mascara

Lips

Liner

Lip Color

Gloss

Notes

Name of Look _____

Evening ○

Daytime ○

Face

Moisturizer
_____

Concealer
_____

Foundation
_____

Highlight/Blush
_____

Eyes

Brows
_____

Eyelid
_____

Liner
_____

Crease
_____

Mascara

Lips

Liner
_____

Lip Color
_____

Gloss
_____

Notes

Name of Look _____

Evening ○

Daytime ○

Face

Moisturizer

Concealer

Foundation

Highlight/Blush

Eyes

Brows

Eyelid

Liner

Crease

Mascara

Lips

Liner

Lip Color

Gloss

Notes

Name of Look _____

Evening ○

Daytime ○

Face

Moisturizer

_____

Concealer

_____

Foundation

_____

Highlight/Blush

_____

Eyes

Brows

_____

Eyelid

_____

Liner

_____

Crease

_____

Mascara

Lips

Liner

_____

Lip Color

_____

Gloss

_____

Notes

www.ingramcontent.com/pod-product-compliance
Lightning Source LLC
Chambersburg PA
CBHW080543220526

45466CB00010B/3011